The best Crock Pot

Cookbook

50 Mouth-Watering Recipes For Busy People On A Budget. Start Your Journey With Amazing Dishes And Begin To Lose Weight And Regain Confidence

Clara Smith

Table of Contents

Introduction

The crockpot has long been a favorite kitchen implement for the 'set-it-and-forget-it' meal. It's a wonderful invention by whoever thought it up, and it has saved many a few dollars on electricity by not needing to keep the stove and oven on for extended hours and all day. So, what really is a crockpot?

A crockpot is also called a slow cooker or a casserole crockpot. These nicknames refer to the same kitchen appliance, and it is one of the most used reheating methods today. It is basically a cooker with a glazed ceramic bowl that has a tight sealing lid. It is because of the liquid that will go in with the food. The crockpot is then plugged into an electrical socket in the kitchen for it to work.

The crockpot slow cooking method involves basically depositing the ingredients you desire to cook into the crockpot bowl (usually by stirring it with a wooden spoon or a ladle), adding the liquid of choice, cooking it for a few hours until it's done. These used to be the standard cooking methods in kitchens, and they have stayed the same with the invention of the crockpot. Nowadays, most crockpots have interiors thermostatically controlled to ensure that it's set at the right temperature during the cooking process to not over-cook your meals.

The best in crockpot slow cooking is finding that low and slow recipe. Recipes that are low in time length are usually very low in steps, and not much work is involved. It usually leads to the much sought after 'set it and forget it' kind of meal. Imagine not having to watch your meals cook slowly as you work on other tasks; you can avoid the temptation of peeking or checking on it too often and not having to worry about burning or crusting on the sides of your crockpot. When cooking at low heat, you don't have to worry about your meal exploding all over the kitchen or all the grease falling out and sticking to the bottom of your crock.

The best use of crockpot slow cooking is the convenience of the food, especially during holidays and parties. You can set the crockpot down on the table, and everyone can serve themselves. It is an excellent and great way to spend time with your guests and treat them well. There is nothing cheesier than eating the same dish fondue style. You get to enjoy slow cooking hotdogs for hours and hours without little ones surreptitiously taking off the top and poaching them in the pool of oil sitting beside the dish.

A crockpot is a very good way to use leftovers for a delicious meal. If you cook a large meal regularly and you have leftovers, put them in a crockpot with a liquid and let it cook. It will double the amount of food leftover or fed to the cat at the end of the week.

Crockpot cooking generally saves time, but it is also a low-budget way to cook. Slow cooking food can save you money because they are usually very low and easy to make. In fact, it is even possible to cook a meal with the last few pennies in your wallet. If you're on a tight budget and you don't have much to spend on your meals, the crockpot is the way to go.

Crockpots even make for a great gift since it's made in many shapes and sizes, from the really small, 1-quart crockpot to the huge 8 quarts or more. Any shape or size would be a welcome gift for anyone because everyone eats. Any occasion could be a good time to give someone a crockpot, and the more occasions you can name, the more crockpots you could make as gifts.

Crockpots are a good thing for singles who do not have many friends, and getting together can be difficult. You can go on cooking and not having to worry about cooking for anyone. You also don't have to go through the motions of doing a dinner party or charity work every week. You could just throw some ingredients together in your crockpot, turn it on and leave. That way, you're free to do whatever you like while your crockpot cooks your meal.

CHAPTER 1:

Breakfast

1. Ham and Cauliflower "Tater Tots" Casserole

Preparation time: 15 minutesCooking time: 10-12 hours

Servings: 4 Ingredients:

- 1/3 cup almond milk

- 4 eggs

- 1/2 cup shredded Cheddar cheese

- 1/3 cup green bell pepper, diced

- 1/3 pound diced ham

- 1/3 cup chopped onion

- 2/3 pound cauliflower

Directions:

1. Add or layer the ingredients in a crock pot starting with tater torts, then ham, onions, green pepper and finally the cheese. Make another two layers from taters to cheese.

2. Beat eggs and milk in a separate bowl. Season the egg mixture with salt and pepper. Then pour the mixture over the ingredients in the crock pot. Cover and cook for 10-12 hours on low heat.

Nutrition:

Calories 206.3

Fat 11.4g

Carbs 8.1g

Protein 18.3g

2.   Scrambled Eggs with Smoked Salmon

Preparation time: 15 minutes

Cooking time: 2 hours

Servings: 6

Ingredients:

- ¼ lb. smoked salmon

- 12 eggs, fresh

- ½ cup heavy cream

- ¼ cup almond flour

- Salt and black pepper at will

- 2 tbsp Butter

- fresh chives at will

Directions:

1. Cut the slices of salmon. Set aside for garnish. Chop the rest of salmon into small pieces. Take a medium bowl, whisk the eggs and cream together.

2. Add a half of the chopped chives, season eggs with salt and pepper. Add flour. Melt the butter over medium heat and pour into the mixture

3. Spray the inside of the Crock Pot with oil or cooking spray. Add salmon pieces to the mixture, pour everything into the Crock Pot.

4. Cover the lid and put on low for 2 hours. Garnish the dish with remaining salmon, chives. Serve warm and enjoy!

Nutrition:

Calories: 387

Carbs: 6g

Fat: 30g

Protein: 23g

3.   Garlic-Parmesan Asparagus

Preparation time: 15 minutes

Cooking time: 1 hour

Servings: 6

Ingredients:

- 2 tbsp olive oil extra virgin

- 2 tsp minced garlic

- 1 egg, fresh

- ½ tsp garlic salt

- 12 oz fresh asparagus

- 1/3 cup Parmesan cheese

- Pepper at will

Directions:

1. Peel the garlic and mince it. Wash the asparagus. Shred the Parmesan cheese. Take a medium-sized bowl combine oil, garlic, cracked egg, and salt together. Whisk everything well.

2. Cover the green beans and coat them well. Spread the cooking spray over the bottom of the Crock Pot, put the coated asparagus, season with the shredded cheese. Toss everything finely.

3. Cover and cook on high for 1 hour. Once the time is over you may also season with the rest of the cheese. Bon Appetite!

Nutrition:

Calories: 110

Carbs: 10g

Fat: 5g

Protein: 9g

4.   Persian Omelet

Preparation time: 15 minutes

Cooking time: 3 hours & 15 minutes

Servings: 14

Ingredients:

- 2 tbsp olive oil

- 1 tbsp butter

- 1 red onion, large

- 4 green onions

- 2 garlic, cloves

- 2 oz spinach

- ¼ cup fresh chives

- ¼ cup cilantro leaves

- ¼ cup parsley leaves

- 2 tbsp fresh dill

- Kosher salt and black pepper at will

- ¼ cup pine nuts

- 9 eggs, large

- ¼ cup whole milk

- 1 cup Greek yogurt at will

Directions:

1. Peel the onion cut thinly. Chop carefully green onions. Chop chives. Wash spinach after this carefully chops it.

2. Peel garlic and mince. Finely cut cilantro and parsley, dill. Take a saucepan melt the butter. Add red onion, stirring occasionally, it takes about 8-9 minutes.

3. Add green onions, garlic, continue cooking for 4 minutes. Put the spinach, chives, parsley, cilantro, add salt and pepper at will. Remove the skillet, add the pine nuts.

4. Take a bowl, crack the eggs, add milk and a little pepper and whisk. Mix the eggs with veggie mixture.

5. Open the Crock Pot and spread the cooking spray over the bottom and sides. Pour the mix into the Crock Pot.

6. Cover the lid and put on low for 3 hours. Serve with Greek yogurt. Bon Appetite!

Nutrition:

Calories: 220

Carbs: 9g

Fat: 16g

Protein: 12g

5.   Broccoli and Cheese Stuffed Squash

Preparation time: 15 minutes

Cooking time: 3 hours & 15 minutes

Servings: 7

Ingredients:

- 1 squash

- 2 cups broccoli florets

- 3 Garlic

- 1 tsp red pepper flake

- 1 tsp Italian seasoning

- ½ cup mozzarella cheese

- 1/3 cup Parmesan

- cooking spray

- salt and pepper at will

Directions:

1. Wash and dry with a paper towel the squash. Cut in two halves. Take off the seeds. Set aside. Wash broccoli thoroughly and cut into florets. Peel garlic and mince it.

2. Spread the spray over the bottom and the sides of the Crock Pot. Put the halves in the Crock Pot. Add a little bit water of room temperature to the bottom of the Crock Pot.

3. Cover the Crock Pot and put on low for about 2 hours, until squash is mild. Check the readiness once the time is over. Take off the squash and let it cool for about 15 minutes.

4. Take a medium skillet, add pepper flakes and a little bit oil and cook for 20 seconds, stir it constantly. Add broccoli, minced garlic to the skillet, continue to stir thoroughly, until the broccoli is tender.

5. Take the squash (previously cooled) and using a fork, take off the flesh of the squash. Add it to the medium bowl and conjoin with the broccoli mixture.

6. Shred carefully the Parmesan cheese, join salt and pepper at will, add seasoning to the mixture. Mix everything well and fill the squash.

7. Put the filled squash again in the Crock Pot, dress with mozzarella cheese each squash half. Add a little bit water if needed to the bottom of the Crock Pot.

8. Cover and cook on low for about 1 hour. Remove the dish and enjoy! Bon Appetite!

Nutrition:

Calories: 314

Carbs: 39g

Fat: 11g

Protein: 21g

CHAPTER 2:

Mains

6.   Chicken Chili

Preparation time: 10 minutes

Cooking time: 6 hours

Servings: 8

Ingredients:

- 1 Tablespoon butter

- 1 red onion, sliced

- 1 bell pepper, sliced

- 2 garlic cloves, minced

- 3 pounds boneless chicken thighs

- 8 slices bacon, chopped

- 1 teaspoon chili powder

- Salt and pepper to taste

- 1 cup chicken broth

- ¼ cup coconut milk

- 3 Tablespoons tomato paste

Directions:

1. Add all ingredients to the crock-pot, starting with the butter. Cover, cook on low for 6 hours. Shred the chicken with a fork in the crock-pot. Serve.

Nutrition:

Calories: 210

Carbs: 32g

Fat: 4g

Protein: 14g

7.   Beef Shoulder in BBQ Sauce

Preparation time: 15 minutes

Cooking time: 10 hours

Servings: 12

Ingredients:

- 8 pounds beef shoulder, whole

- 1 Tablespoon butter

- 1 yellow onion, diced

- 1 garlic bulb, peeled and minced

- 4 Tablespoons red wine vinegar

- 2 Tablespoons Worcestershire sauce

- 4 Tablespoons Swerve (or suitable substitute)

- 1 Tablespoon mustard

- 1 teaspoon salt

- 1 teaspoon fresh ground black pepper

Directions:

1. In a bowl, mix seasoning together. Set aside. In a pan, melt the butter, add the meat. Brown on all sides. Transfer to crock-pot.

2. In the same pan, fry the onion for 2-3 minutes, pour over the meat. Pour in the seasoning. Cover, cook on low for 10 hours.

3. Remove from crock-pot, place on a platter, cover with foil, let it rest for 1 hour. Turn the crock pot on high, reduce the remaining liquid by half and serve with the shredded beef.

Nutrition:

Calories: 140

Carbs: 5g

Fat: 9g

Protein: 8g

8.   Dressed Pork Leg Roast

Preparation time: 5 minutes

Cooking time: 8 hours

Servings: 14

Ingredients:

- 8 pounds pork leg

- 1 Tablespoon butter

- 1 yellow onion, sliced

- 6 garlic cloves, peeled and minced

- 2 Tablespoons ground cumin

- 2 Tablespoons ground thyme

- 2 Tablespoons ground chili

- 1 teaspoon salt

- 1 teaspoon fresh ground black pepper

- 1 cup hot water

Directions:

1. Butter the crock-pot. Slice crisscrosses along top of pork leg. Arrange onion slices and minced garlic along the bottom of the crock-pot. Place meat on top of vegetables.

2. In a small bowl, mix the herbs. Rub it all over the pork leg. Add the water. Cover, cook on high for 8 hours.

3. Remove from crock pot, place on a platter, cover with foil. Let it rest for 1 hour. Shred the meat and serve.

Nutrition:

Calories: 143

Carbs: 0g

Fat: 3g

Protein: 28g

9. Rabbit & Mushroom Stew

Preparation time: 10 minutes

Cooking time: 6 hours

Servings: 6

Ingredients:

- 1 rabbit, in portion size pieces

- 2 cups spicy Spanish sausage, cut in chunks

- 2 Tablespoons butter, divided

- 1 red onion, sliced

- 1 cup button mushrooms, washed and dried

- 1 teaspoon cayenne pepper

- 1 teaspoon sweet paprika

- 1 teaspoon salt

- 1 teaspoon fresh ground black pepper

- 1 cup chicken broth+1 cup hot water

Directions:

1. Butter the crock-pot. In a large pan, melt the butter, add the pieces of rabbit, brown on all sides. Transfer to crock-pot.

2. In the same pan, sauté the onions, sausage chunks, and spices for 2-3 minutes. Pour in chicken broth to deglaze the pan, heat on high for 1 minute then pour the mixture over the rabbit.

3. Add the mushrooms. Adjust the seasoning, if needed. Add the water. Cover, cook on high for 6 hours. Serve.

Nutrition:

Calories: 189

Carbs: 20g

Fat: 6g

Protein: 13g

CHAPTER 3:

Sides

10. Spinach and Squash Side Salad

Preparation time: 15 minutes

Cooking time: 4 hours

Servings: 4

Ingredients:

- 3 pounds butternut squash, peeled and cubed

- 1 yellow onion, chopped

- 2 teaspoons thyme, chopped

- 3 garlic cloves, minced

- A pinch of salt and black pepper

- 10 oz. veggie stock

- 6 oz. baby spinach

Directions:

1. In your crock pot, mix squash cubes with onion, thyme, salt, pepper, and stock, stir, cover, and cook on low for 4 hours. Transfer squash mixture to a bowl, add spinach, toss, divide between plates and serve as a side dish.

Nutrition:

Calories: 100

Fat: 1g

Carbs: 18g

Protein: 4g

11.   **Cheddar Potatoes Mix**

Preparation time: 15 minutes

Cooking time: 3 hours

Servings: 2 people

Ingredients:

- ½ pound gold potatoes, cut into wedges

- 2 oz. heavy cream

- ½ teaspoon turmeric powder

- ½ teaspoon rosemary, dried

- ¼ cup cheddar cheese, shredded

- 1 tablespoon butter, melted

- Cooking spray

- A pinch of salt and black pepper

Directions:

1. Grease your crock pot with the cooking spray, add the potatoes, cream, turmeric, and the rest of the fixing, toss, put the lid on and cook on high for 3 hours. Divide between plates and serve as a side dish.

Nutrition:

Calories: 300

Fat: 14g

Carbs: 22g

Protein: 6g

12.   Cauliflower Pilaf

Preparation time: 15 minutes

Cooking time: 3 hours

Servings: 4

Ingredients:

- 1 cup cauliflower rice

- 6 green onions, chopped

- 3 tablespoons ghee, melted

- 2 garlic cloves, minced

- ½ pound Portobello mushrooms, sliced

- 2 cups warm water

- Salt and black pepper to the taste

Directions:

1. In your crock pot, mix cauliflower rice with green onions, melted ghee, garlic, mushrooms, water, salt, and pepper, stir

well, cover, and cook on low for 3 hours. Divide between plates and serve as a side dish.

Nutrition:

Calories: 200

Fat: 5g

Carbs: 14g

Protein: 4g

13.   Cinnamon Squash

Preparation time: 15 minutes

Cooking time: 4 hours

Servings: 2 people

Ingredients:

- 1 acorn squash, peeled and cut into medium wedges

- 1 cup coconut cream

- A pinch of cinnamon powder

- A bit of salt and black pepper

Directions:

1. In your crock pot, mix the squash with the cream and the rest of the fixing, toss, cook on low within 4 hours. Divide between plates and serve as a side dish.

Nutrition: Calories: 230 Fat: 3g Carbs: 10g Protein: 2g

14.   Broccoli Filling

Preparation time: 15 minutes Cooking time: 5 hours

Servings: 4 Ingredients:

- 10 oz. broccoli, chopped

- 7 oz. Cheddar cheese, shredded

- 4 eggs

- ½ cup onion, chopped

- 1 cup heavy cream

- 3 tbsp mayo sauce

- 3 tbsp butter

- ½ cup bread crumbs

Directions:

1. Spread broccoli in the insert of the crock pot and top it with ½ cup cream. Put the crock pot's lid on and set the cooking time to 3 hours on high.

2. Beat eggs with onion, mayo sauce, butter, and remaining cream in a bowl. Mash the cooked broccoli and stir in the mayo-eggs mixture.

3. Spread the breadcrumbs over the broccoli mixture. Put the crock pot's lid on and set the cooking time to 2 hours on high. Serve warm.

Nutrition:

Calories: 289

Fat: 22.9g

Carbs: 9.07g

Protein: 13g

CHAPTER 4:

Seafood

15.   Fish and Bacon Soup

Preparation time: 15 minutes

Cooking time: 4 hours

Servings: 6

Ingredients:

- 5 slices streaky bacon, chopped

- 4 fillets of fresh white fish, chopped into chunks

- 5 garlic cloves, crushed

- 4 cups fish stock

- 1 cup crème fraiche

Directions:

1. Drizzle some olive oil into the Crock Pot. Add the bacon, fish, garlic, stock, salt, and pepper to the pot, stir to combine.

2. Place the lid onto the pot and set the temperature to high. Cook for 4 hours. Remove the lid and stir the crème fraiche into the soup.

3. Serve with an extra dollop of crème fraiche and some freshly chopped herbs!

Nutrition:

Calories: 260

Carbs: 0g

Fat: 12g

Protein: 0g

16.   Mozzarella Shrimp Parcels

Preparation time: 15 minutes

Cooking time: 3 hours

Servings: 12

Ingredients:

- 2 cups frozen shrimp (thawed)

- 12 slices streaky bacon, cut in half

- 2 cups grated mozzarella cheese

- Large bunch of Kale, washed and hard stalks removed

- 12 small skewers, (or 6 long ones, cut in half)

Directions:

1. Cut the kale into 12 large pieces. On a large board, lay out the kale halves. Lay 2 bacon half slices on the kale. Place a small handful of shrimps on top of the bacon.

2. Place a small handful of grated mozzarellas on top of the shrimp. Sprinkle with salt and pepper. Wrap the parcels up

tightly by folding the sides up, then folding the top and bottom up, and use a skewer to secure them.

3. Drizzle some olive oil into the Crock Pot. Place the parcels into the pot. Place the lid onto the pot and set the temperature to high. Cook for 3 hours.

4. Heat some olive oil into a frying pan. Take the parcels out of the Crock Pot once cooked and transfer them to the hot oil to cook on both sides to create a crisp and golden outer.

5. Serve with your choice of sauces and dips!

Nutrition:

Calories: 323

Carbs: 20g

Fat: 10g

Protein: 35g

17.   Coconut Lime Mussels

Preparation time: 15 minutes

Cooking time: 2 hours & 30 minutes

Servings: 4

Ingredients:

- 16 fresh mussels

- 4 garlic cloves

- 1 ½ cup full-fat coconut milk

- ½ red chili, finely chopped

- 1 lime

- ½ cup fish stock

- Handful of fresh coriander, chopped

Directions:

1. Drizzle some olive oil into the Crock Pot. Add the garlic, coconut milk, chili, fish stock, salt, pepper, and juice of one lime to the pot, stir to combine.

2. Place the lid onto the pot and set the temperature to high. Cook for 2 hours. Remove the lid, place the mussels into the liquid and place the lid back onto the pot.

3. Cook for about 20 minutes, or until the mussels open. Serve while hot, with a generous serving of coconut and lime sauce over the top, and a big handful of fresh coriander!

Nutrition:

Calories: 302

Carbs: 21g

Fat: 13g

Protein: 33g

18.   Calamari, Prawn, And Shrimp "Pasta" Sauce

Preparation time: 15 minutes

Cooking time: 3 hours

Servings: 5

Ingredients:

- 1 cup calamari

- 1 cup prawns

- 1 cup shrimp

- 6 garlic cloves, crushed

- 4 tomatoes, chopped

- 1 tsp dried mixed herbs

- 1 tbsp balsamic vinegar

Directions:

1. Drizzle some olive oil into the Crock Pot. Add the calamari, prawns, shrimp, garlic, tinned tomatoes, mixed herbs, balsamic vinegar, salt, and pepper, stir to combine.

2.   Place the lid onto the pot and set the temperature to high. Cook for 3 hours. Serve with zucchini noodles or a side of fresh veggies!

Nutrition:

Calories: 355

Carbs: 42g

Fat: 12g

Protein: 20g

19.   Whole Fish with Ginger and Soy

Preparation time: 15 minutes

Cooking time: 2 hours

Servings: 4

Ingredients:

- 1 fresh, whole fish

- 4 garlic cloves, crushed

- 2 tbsp grated fresh ginger

- 4 tbsp soy sauce

Directions:

1. Score the fish with a sharp knife by cutting diagonal lines through the skin. Rub the fish with olive oil. Sprinkle the fish with sea salt and pepper.

2. Sprinkle the grated ginger onto the fish and rub it into the scores. Drizzle some olive oil into the Crock Pot. Place the fish into the pot.

3. Pour the soy sauce over top of the fish. Place the lid onto the pot and set the temperature to high. Cook for 2 hours. Serve immediately! Garnish with fresh green herbs to give a pop of color.

Nutrition:

Calories: 430

Carbs: 25g

Fat: 6g

Protein: 68g

CHAPTER 5:

Poultry

20.   Mango Pineapple Chicken Tacos

Preparation time: 15 minutes

Cooking time: 5-6 hours

Servings: 16

Ingredients:

- 2 medium mangoes, peeled and chopped

- 1½ cups cubed fresh pineapple or canned pineapple chunks, drained

- 2 medium tomatoes, chopped

- 1 medium red onion, finely chopped

- 2 small Anaheim peppers, deseeded and chopped

- 2 green onions, finely chopped

- 1 tablespoon lime juice

- 1 teaspoon sugar

- 4 pounds (1.8 kg) bone-in chicken breast halves, skin removed

- 3 teaspoons salt

- ¼ cup packed brown sugar

- 32 taco shells, warmed

- ¼ cup minced fresh cilantro

Directions:

1. In a large bowl, combine the first eight ingredients. Place chicken in a crock pot; sprinkle with salt and brown sugar.

2. Top with mango mixture. Cover and cook on low for 5 to 6 hours or until chicken is tender.

3. Remove chicken; cool slightly. Strain cooking juices, reserving mango mixture and ½ cup juices. Discard remaining juices.

When cool enough to handle, remove chicken from bones; discard bones.

4. Shred chicken with two forks. Return chicken and reserved mango mixture and cooking juices to crock pot; heat through. Serve in taco shells; sprinkle with cilantro.

Nutrition:

Calories: 246

Carbs: 25g

Fat: 7g

Protein: 21g

21. Mushroom Chicken Alfredo

Preparation time: 15 minutes

Cooking time: 4-5 hours

Servings: 4

Ingredients:

- 4 bone-in chicken breast halves (12 to 14 ounces / 340 to 397 g each), skin removed

- 2 tablespoons canola oil

- 1 (305-g) can condensed cream of chicken soup, undiluted

- 1 (305-g) can condensed cream of mushroom soup, undiluted

- 1 cup chicken broth

- 1 small onion, chopped

- 1 (170-g) jar sliced mushrooms, drained

- ¼ teaspoon garlic salt

- ¼ teaspoon pepper

- 8 ounces (227 g) fettuccine

- 1 (227-g) package cream cheese, softened and cubed

- Shredded Parmesan cheese (optional)

Directions:

1. In a large skillet, brown chicken in oil in batches. Transfer to a crock pot. In a large bowl, combine the soups, broth, onion, mushrooms, garlic salt and pepper; pour over meat.

2. Cover and cook on low for 4 to 5 hours or until chicken is tender. Cook fettuccine according to package directions; drain.

3. Remove chicken from crock pot and keep warm. Turn crock pot off and stir in cream cheese until melted. Serve with fettucine. Top with Parmesan cheese if desired.

Nutrition:

Calories: 462

Carbs: 33g

Fat: 26g Protein: 21g

22. Jamaican-Inspired Brown Chicken Stew

Preparation time: 15 minutesCooking time: 6-8 hours

Servings: 8 Ingredients:

- ¼ cup ketchup

- 3 garlic cloves, minced

- 1 tablespoon sugar

- 1 tablespoon hot pepper sauce

- 1 teaspoon browning sauce (optional)

- 1 teaspoon dried basil

- 1 teaspoon dried thyme

- 1 teaspoon paprika

- ½ teaspoon salt

- ½ teaspoon dried oregano

- ½ teaspoon ground allspice

- ½ teaspoon pepper

- 8 bone-in chicken thighs (about 3 pounds / 1.4 kg), skin removed

- 1 pound (454 g) fully cooked andouille chicken sausage links, sliced 1 medium onion, finely chopped

- 2 medium carrots, finely chopped

- 2 celery ribs, finely chopped

Directions:

1. In a large resealable plastic bag, combine ketchup, garlic, sugar, pepper sauce and, if desired, browning sauce; stir in seasonings.

2. Add chicken thighs, sausage and vegetables. Seal bag and turn to coat. Refrigerate 8 hours or overnight. Transfer contents of bag to a crock pot. Cook, covered, on low 6 to 8 hours or until chicken is tender.

Nutrition:

Calories: 235 Carbs: 9g

Fat: 9g

Protein: 28g

23.   **Lemon-Dill Chicken**

Preparation time: 15 minutes

Cooking time: 4-5 hours

Servings: 6

Ingredients:

- 2 medium onions, coarsely chopped

- 2 tablespoons butter, softened

- ¼ teaspoon grated lemon peel

- 1 broiler/fryer chicken (4 to 5 pounds / 1.8 to 2.3 kg)

- ¼ cup chicken stock

- 4 sprigs fresh parsley

- 4 fresh dill sprigs

- 3 tablespoons lemon juice

- 1 teaspoon salt

- 1 teaspoon paprika

- ½ teaspoon dried thyme

- ¼ teaspoon pepper

Directions:

1. Place onions on the bottom of a crock pot. In a small bowl, mix butter and lemon peel. Tuck wings under chicken; tie drumsticks together.

2. With fingers, carefully loosen skin from chicken breast; rub butter mixture under the skin. Secure skin to underside of breast with toothpicks. Place chicken over onions, breast side up. Add stock, parsley and dill.

3. Drizzle lemon juice over the chicken; sprinkle with seasonings. Cook, covered, on low 4 to 5 hours. Remove chicken from crock pot; tent with foil. Let stand 15 minutes before carving.

Nutrition:

Calories: 173

Carbs: 3g

Fat: 6g Protein: 24g

24.   **Cornbread Chicken Bake**

Preparation time: 15 minutes

Cooking time: 3-4 hours

Servings: 6

Ingredients:

- 5 cups cubed cornbread

- ¼ cup butter, cubed

- 1 large onion, chopped (about 2 cups)

- 4 celery ribs, chopped (about 2 cups)

- 3 cups shredded cooked chicken

- 1 (10¾-ounce / 305-g) can condensed cream of chicken soup, undiluted

- 1 (10¾-ounce / 305-g) can condensed cream of mushroom soup, undiluted

- ½ cup reduced-sodium chicken broth

- 1 teaspoon poultry seasoning

- ½ teaspoon salt

- ½ teaspoon rubbed sage

- ¼ teaspoon pepper

Directions:

1. Preheat oven to 350°F (180°C). Place bread cubes on an ungreased 15x10-in. baking pan. Bake 20 to 25 minutes or until toasted. Cool on baking pan.

2. In a large skillet, heat butter over medium-high heat. Add onion and celery; cook and stir 6 to 8 minutes or until tender.

3. Transfer to a greased crock pot. Stir in corn bread, chicken, soups, broth and seasonings. Cook, covered, on low 3 to 4 hours or until heated through.

Nutrition:Calories: 478 Carbs: 36g Fat: 21g Protein: 35g

CHAPTER 6:

Meat

25.   Corned Beef and Cabbage

Preparation time: 15 minutes

Cooking time: 6 hours

Servings: 12

Ingredients:

- 6 lb. corned beef brisket

- 4 medium-sized carrots, peeled and cut into bite-size pieces

- 8 cups shredded cabbage

- 1 corned beef spiced packet

- 6 cups water

Directions:

1. Rub the meat with the corned beef spice packet. Grease a 4-quart crock pot with a non-stick cooking spray and add the carrots and the cabbage.

2. Pour in water, then top with the seasoned beef. Cover the crock pot with its lid, and set the cooking timer for 6 hours allowing to cook at a low heat. Serve the meat immediately, with the vegetables alongside.

Nutrition:

Calories: 334

Carbohydrates: 8.1 g

Fats: 22.8 g

Protein: 24.7 g

26. Ancho-Beef Stew

Preparation time: 15 minutes

Cooking time: 10 hours & 7 minutes

Servings: 4

Ingredients:

- 8 oz boneless beef chuck pot roast, trimmed

- 16 oz low-carb vegetables

- 1 tablespoon ground ancho-chili pepper

- 12 oz tomato salsa, sugar-free

- 1 1/2 cups of beef broth

Directions:

1. Cut meat into bite-size pieces and season on all sides with the ancho-chili pepper. Place a large non-stick skillet pan over medium-high heat, add 1 tablespoon olive oil, then the seasoned beef.

2. Allow to cook for 5 to 7 minutes, or until browned on all sides. Depending on the size of your pan, you can cook the beef chunks in batches.

3. Grease a 4-quart crock pot with a non-stick cooking spray and add the vegetables. Top with the browned meat and season with salt and ground black pepper.

4. Stir in the tomato salsa and the beef broth, then cover the crock pot with its lid. Set the cooking timer for 8 to 10 hours, allowing the meat to cook at a low heat setting or until meat is cooked through. Serve the meat warm, with the vegetables alongside.

Nutrition:

Calories: 288

Carbohydrates: 8 g

Fats: 20 g

Protein: 20 g

27.   Cider Braised Beef Pot Roast

Preparation time: 15 minutes

Cooking time: 8 hours & 10 minutes

Servings: 4

Ingredients:

- 8 oz boneless chuck pot roast, trimmed

- 1/2 cup chopped white onion

- 1 teaspoon garlic powder

- 1/4 cup apple cider vinegar

- 1/4 teaspoon xanthan gum

Directions:

1. Season the chuck roast with the garlic powder, salt, and ground black pepper. Place a large non-stick skillet pan over medium-high heat, add a tablespoon of olive oil, then add the meat.

2. Allow to cook for 7 to 10 minutes, turning until it has browned on all sides. Grease a 4-quart crock pot with a non-stick cooking spray and add the browned meat.

3. Top with the onion and pour in the vinegar and 1 1/2 cups of water. Cover the crock pot with its lid, and set the cooking timer for 8 hours, allowing the meat to cook at a low heat setting.

4. Place the meat on a plate, then shred using forks, and keep warm. Transfer the remaining mixture to a saucepan, add the xanthan gum, and bring to boil, allowing to cook until sauce reduces to the desired thickness. Serve the meat with the sauce alongside.

Nutrition:

Calories: 393

Carbohydrates: 4 g

Fats: 28 g

Protein: 30 g

28. Cajun Pot Roast

Preparation time: 15 minutes

Cooking time: 8 hours

Servings: 8

Ingredients:

- 18 oz boneless beef chuck roast, trimmed

- 1 white onion, peeled and chopped

- 14 oz diced tomatoes with garlic,

- 1 tablespoon Cajun seasoning,

- 1 teaspoon Tabasco sauce

Directions:

1. Season the beef on all sides with the Cajun seasoning mix. Grease a 4-quart crock pot with a non-stick cooking spray, add the seasoned beef, and top with the onion.

2. In a bowl, stir together the tomato with garlic, the Tabasco sauce and a pinch of salt and ground black pepper. Pour the tomato

mixture over the vegetables and beef, then cover the crock pot with its lid.

3. Set the cooking timer for 6 to 8 hours, and allow to cook at a low heat setting. To serve, transfer the beef to a serving platter, then top with onion and tomato mixture.

Nutrition:

Calories: 314 Kcal

Carbohydrates: 10.4 g

Fats: 15.1 g

Protein: 38 g

29.   Sloppy Joes

Preparation time: 15 minutes

Cooking time: 8 hours & 10 minutes

Servings: 6

Ingredients:

- 1 lb. ground beef

- 2 tablespoons Worcestershire sauce

- 1 tablespoon Dijon mustard

- 1 cup Picante Sauce, sugar-free

- 3/4 cup hot barbecue sauce, sugar-free

Directions:

1. Place a large non-stick skillet pan over medium-high heat, and add the beef. Cook for 8 to 10 minutes, stirring regularly, until the meat is no longer pink.

2. Drain the fat from the mixture, and transfer to a 4-quart crock pot. Stir in the remaining ingredients, and season with salt and black pepper.

3. Seal the crock pot with its lid, then set the cooking timer for 6 to 8 hours, allow the mixture to cook at a low heat setting.

4. To serve, place a generous helping of the mixture on a roasted Portobello mushroom caps, and top with a second Portobello mushroom cap.

Nutrition:

Calories: 162.5

Carbohydrates: 2.5 g

Fats: 4.5 g

Protein: 24 g

CHAPTER 7:

Vegetables

30. Cheese Sauced Cauliflower & Broccoli

Preparation time: 15 minutes

Cooking time: 6-7 hours

Servings: 10

Ingredients:

- 4 cups broccoli florets

- 4 cups cauliflower florets

- 1 chopped onion

- 14 oz. alfredo pasta sauce

- 6 oz. processed Swiss cheese

- 1 tsp. thyme, dry

- ¼ tsp. black pepper

- ½ cup Sliced almonds

Directions:

1. In a crock pot, mix all the above ingredients except the almonds. Cook covered for 6-7 hours on low. Stir gently and serve garnished with almonds.

Nutrition:

Calories: 177

Fat: 12 g

Carbs: 10 g

Protein: 8 g

31. Low Carb Cabbage Rolls

Preparation time: 15 minutes

Cooking time: 4 hours

Servings: 2

Ingredients:

- 2 cloves Garlic, minced

- ½ diced Onion

- 794 g Artichoke hearts, chopped

- 283 g chopped Spinach

- 283 g chopped Kale

- 1 cup Parmesan cheese

- 1 cup shredded Mozzarella cheese

- 1 cup plain Greek yogurt

- ¾ cup Sour cream

- ¼ cup low fat Mayonnaise

- Salt

- Pepper

Directions:

1. Add all the ingredients and stir in the crock pot. Put high heat to cook for 4 hours. Add salt and pepper for seasoning. Serve.

Nutrition:

Calories: 98

Fat: 2 g

Carbs: 5 g

Protein: 6 g

32. Squash & Zucchini

Preparation time: 15 minutes

Cooking time: 4-6 hours

Servings: 6

Ingredients:

- 2 cups sliced zucchini

- 2 cups sliced yellow squash

- ¼ tsp. Pepper

- 1 tsp. Italian seasoning

- Garlic powder

- ½ tsp. Sea salt

- ¼ cups cubed butter

- ¼ cups grated Parmesan cheese

Directions:

1. In a crock pot, mix all the above ingredients. Cook covered for 4-6 hours on low.

Nutrition:

Calories: 122

Fat: 9.9 g

Carbs: 5.4 g

Protein: 4.2 g

33.　Roasted Vegetable

Preparation time: 15 minutes

Cooking time: 5 hours

Servings: 4

Ingredients:

- 2 sliced bell peppers

- 3 sliced zucchinis

- ½ cup minced garlic

- 1 tbsp. Italian herb mix

- 2 tbsp. olive oil

Directions:

1. Place all ingredients in a mixing bowl. Season with salt if desired. Toss to coat everything. Place in the crock pot and cook on low for 5 hours.

Nutrition: Calories: 96 Carbs: 8.01 g Protein: 1.75 g Fat: 6.91 g

34.   Spaghetti Squash Carbonara

Preparation time: 15 minutes

Cooking time: 8 hours & 10 minutes

Servings: 4

Ingredients:

- 2 cups of water

- 1 3-pound spaghetti squash

- ½ cup coconut bacon

- ½ cup fresh spinach leaves

- 1 egg

- 3 tablespoons heavy cream

- 3 tablespoons unsweetened almond milk

- ½ cup grated Parmesan cheese

- 1 teaspoon garlic powder

- Salt and pepper to taste

Directions:

1. Put squash in your crockpot and pour in 2 cups of water. Close the lid. Cook on low for 8-9 hours. When the spaghetti squash cools, mix egg, cream, milk, and cheese in a bowl.

2. When the squash is cool enough for you to handle with oven mitts, cut it open lengthwise and scrape out noodles. Mix in the egg mixture right away.

3. Add spinach and seasonings. Top with coconut bacon and enjoy!

Nutrition:

Calories: 256

Carbs: 10g

Fat: 19g

Protein: 13g

35.   Summery Bell Pepper + Eggplant Salad

Preparation time: 15 minutes

Cooking time: 7 hours

Servings: 4

Ingredients:

- 1 24-ounce can of whole tomatoes

- 2 sliced yellow bell peppers

- 2 small eggplants (smaller ones tend to be less bitter)

- 1 sliced red onion

- 1 tablespoon paprika

- 2 teaspoons cumin

- Salt and pepper to taste

- A squeeze of lime juice

Directions:

1. Mix all the fixings in your crockpot. Close the lid. Cook on low for 7-8 hours. When time is up, serve warm, or chill in the fridge for a few hours before eating.

Nutrition:

Calories: 197

Carbs: 28g

Fat: 8g

Protein: 7g

36.   Squash Noodles

Preparation time: 15 minutesCooking time: 4 hours

Servings: 4 Ingredients:

- 1-pound butternut squash, seeded, halved

- 1 tablespoon vegan butter

- 1 teaspoon salt

- ½ teaspoon garlic powder

- 1 cup water

Directions:

1. Pour water into the crockpot. Add butternut squash and close the lid. Cook the vegetable on high for 4 hours.

2. Then drain water and shred the squash flesh with the help of the fork, and transfer in the bowl. Add garlic powder, salt, and butter. Mix the squash noodles.

Nutrition: Calories 78 Protein 1.2 g Carbs 13.5 g Fat 3 g

CHAPTER 8:

Soups & Stews

37. Creamy Harvest Pumpkin Bisque

Preparation Time: 15 minutes

Cooking Time: 5 hours

Servings: 8

Ingredients:

- 1 Medium pumpkin (butternut, sugar, etc.)

- 1 medium sweet potato, peeled and diced

- 2 carrots, chopped

- 1 medium yellow onion, chopped

- 2 cups vegetable stock

- 1 tsp curry powder

- ½ tsp ground ginger

- ½ tsp ground nutmeg

- ½ tsp cumin

- 1 cup heavy cream

- Kosher salt

- Freshly ground black pepper

Directions:

1. Peel pumpkin skin, and remove pulp and seeds. Cube up the pumpkin flesh. Place pumpkin, potato, carrots, onion, vegetable stock, and spices in the crockpot.

2. Cook within 4-5 hours, low or 2-3 hours, high. Make sure vegetables are incredibly tender. Pulse in a blender, then return it inside the crockpot and add in the heavy cream, stirring until thoroughly mixed.

3. Season with salt and pepper as desired. Heat back up to desired heat and serve.

Nutrition:

Carbs: 13g

Calories: 125

Fat: 5g

Protein: 2g

38.   Zesty White Chicken Chili

Preparation Time: 15 minutes

Cooking Time: 8 hours

Servings: 6

Ingredients:

- 2 lbs. Boneless, skinless chicken breasts or thighs

- 1 large yellow onion, diced

- 1 medium green bell pepper, chopped

- 1 small jalapeno, minced

- 6 cloves garlic, minced

- 3 tsp. ground cumin (add more to taste)

- 1 tsp. dried oregano

- 2 tsp. chili powder (add more to taste)

- 1 tsp. kosher salt

- ¼ tsp. black pepper

- 6 cups chicken stock

- 1 lime, juiced

- ½ cup fresh cilantro, chopped

- ½ cup chives chopped

Directions:

1. Throw the peppers, jalapeno, onion, garlic, spices into the crockpot. Place the chicken on top and fill with all of the broth.

2. Cook covered on low for 7-8 hours. Check the chicken with a fork to see if it is falling apart. Add the lime juice and stir, add salt and pepper to taste. When serving, top off with cilantro and chives.

Nutrition:

Carbs: 6g

Calories: 105

Fat: 0g

Protein: 25 g

39.   Tuscan Zucchini Stew

Preparation Time: 20 minutes

Cooking Time: 6 hours

Servings: 6

Ingredients:

- 1 1/2 pounds Italian-seasoned sausage (spicy or sweet, whatever you prefer)

- 1 cup celery, chopped small

- 3 cups sliced zucchini, sliced into thin rounds

- 1 green bell pepper, chopped small

- 1 red or yellow bell pepper, chopped

- 1 large onion, diced

- 3 cloves garlic, minced

- ½ tsp. fresh ground black pepper

- 2 teaspoons salt

- 1 (28 oz) can diced tomatoes

- 2 (14 oz) cans of fire-roasted diced tomatoes

- ½ cup water

- 1 teaspoon brown sugar

- 2 teaspoon Italian seasoning

- 1 teaspoon dried basil

- ¼ cup asiago cheese, grated

- Red pepper flakes (optional)

Directions:

1. Fry the sausage on medium heat on the stove. Break up the meat with a spatula and make sure it's fully cooked (5-8 minutes). Drain off the grease.

2. Add the celery, onions and peppers continue to cook until the vegetables become soft and translucent (7-8 minutes).

3. Add minced garlic and cook and stir continually until fragrant (2 minutes) Add the salt and pepper, stir and remove from the heat. Pour sausage mixture into the crockpot.

4. Put the 3 cans of diced tomatoes, the spices, the sugar, and the water. Cook on low for 4-6 hours. Top with grated asiago, and add a fresh sprig of basil (optional).

Nutrition:

Calories: 280

Carbs: 16g

Fat: 22g

Protein: 23g

40.   Mexican Chorizo Enchilada Soup

Preparation Time: 15 minutes Cooking Time: 4 hours

Servings: 8

Ingredients:

- 1 lb. ground beef

- 1 lb. chorizo sausage

- 2 (8oz.) packages Neufchâtel (cream) cheese

- 2 cans of roasted tomatoes, dice

- 1 medium jalapeno, chopped finely

- 1 large onion, chopped

- 1 clove of garlic, minced

- 1 green bell pepper, chopped

- 1 (1.25 oz) package taco seasoning (or more to taste)

- 4 cups of chicken stock

- ¼ cup fresh cilantro

- ¼ cup shredded sharp cheddar cheese (optional)

- Low-fat Sour cream (optional)

Directions:

1. Heat-up a large skillet, and brown the beef and chorizo over medium heat. Break the meat up until crumbly with a spatula.

2. Stir in onion, jalapeno, and bell pepper. Cook until onions start to soften (5-7 minutes). Put the garlic and continue to stir and cook for 2 more minutes. Sprinkle the taco seasoning packet over the meat mixture and stir.

3. Put the meat batter inside the crockpot and add the Neufchâtel cheese and canned tomatoes. Stir until the cheese breaks down and mixes in.

4. Cook within 4 hours, low or high for 2 hours. Put the cilantro and cook for another 10-15 minutes. Garnish with cheddar cheese and sour cream, and serve.

Nutrition: Calories: 531 Carbs: 7g Fat: 42 g Protein: 28g

41.   Chicken Soup with Veggie Noodles

Preparation Time: 15 minutes Cooking Time: 8 hours

Servings: 8 Ingredients:

- 1 1/2 lbs. boneless chicken breast, cubes

- 2 cups carrots, sliced into thin rounds

- 1 large yellow onion, diced

- 3 stalks celery, chopped

- 4 cloves garlic, minced

- 3 tbsp. extra virgin olive oil

- 1/2 tsp Italian seasoning

- ¼ tsp dried parsley

- 6 cups chicken stock

- 1 cup water

- ½ tsp kosher salt

- ¼ tsp. freshly ground black pepper

- 2 Medium-sized zucchinis

- 2 cups chopped Napa cabbage

Directions:

1. Place all ingredients except cabbage and zucchini into the crockpot. Stir until evenly mixed. Cook on low for 6-8 hours.

2. In the last 2 hours of cooking, take the zucchini, and make Zucchini noodles. If you do not have a veggie noodle machine, take a potato peeler and peel the zucchini, then use the peeler to shave off thin strips of zucchini.

3. Take the zucchini noodles and the chopped cabbage and sauté in a large skillet over medium heat with extra virgin olive oil.

4. Stir occasionally as the vegetables soften, and the cabbage starts to caramelize and brown a little bit (about 7-8 minutes).

5. Put the vegetables inside the crockpot, then continue to cook for the remaining 1-2 hours, then serve.

Nutrition: Calories: 145 Carbs: 7g Fat: 6g Protein: 20g

CHAPTER 9:

Snacks

42.   Candied Walnuts

Preparation Time: 10 minutes

Cooking Time: 2¼ hours

Servings: 16

Ingredients:

- ½ cup unsalted butter

- 1 pound walnuts

- ½ cup Splenda, granular

- 1½ teaspoons ground cinnamon

- ¼ teaspoon ground allspice

- ¼ teaspoon ground ginger

- 1/8 teaspoon ground cloves

Directions:

1. Set a crockpot on High and preheat for about 15 minutes. In preheated crockpot, add butter and walnuts and stir to combine.

2. Add the Splenda and stir to combine well. Cook, covered, for about 15 minutes. Uncover the crockpot and stir the mixture.

3. Now, set the crockpot on Low and cook, uncovered, for about 2 hours, stirring occasionally. Transfer the walnuts to a bowl.

4. In another small bowl, mix together spices. Sift spice mixture over walnuts and toss to coat evenly. Set aside to cool before serving.

Nutrition:

Calories: 227

Carbohydrates: 10.5g

Protein: 6.9g Fat: 22.5g

43. Flavorful Pecans

Preparation Time: 20 minutes

Cooking Time: 2¼ hours

Servings: 16

Ingredients:

- 1 pound pecan halves

- ¼ cup butter, melted

- 1 teaspoon dried oregano

- 1 teaspoon dried basil

- 1 teaspoon dried thyme

- 1 tablespoon red chili powder

- ½ teaspoon onion powder

- ¼ teaspoon garlic powder

- ¼ teaspoon cayenne pepper

- Salt, to taste

Directions:

1. In a large crockpot, add all ingredients and stir to combine. Set the crockpot on High and cook, covered, for about 15 minutes.

2. Uncover the crockpot and stir the mixture. Now, set the crockpot on Low and cook, uncovered, for about 2 hours, stirring occasionally. Transfer the pecans into a bowl and keep aside to cool before serving.

Nutrition:

Calories: 225

Carbohydrates: 4.5g

Protein: 3.2g

Fat: 23.2g

44.   Herb Flavored Almonds

Preparation Time: 10 minutes Cooking Time: 2 hours

Servings: 16 Ingredients:

- 2 cups raw almonds

- 1 tablespoon olive oil

- 1 tablespoon dried rosemary

- 1 tablespoon dried thyme

- Salt and freshly ground black pepper, to taste

Directions:

1. In a large crockpot, add all ingredients and stir to combine. Set the crockpot on High and cook, covered, for about 1½ hours, stirring after every 30 minutes.

2. Transfer the almonds into a bowl and set aside to cool before serving.

Nutrition:Calories: 77 Carbohydrates: 2.8g Protein: 2.5g

Fat: 6.9g

45.   Ultra-Spicy Almonds

Preparation Time: 10 minutes Cooking Time: 2½ hours

Servings: 32

Ingredients:

- 2½ tablespoons coconut oil

- 4 cups raw almonds

- 3 garlic cloves, minced

- 1 teaspoon smoked paprika

- 2 teaspoons red chili powder

- 1 teaspoon ground cumin

- 1 teaspoon onion powder

- Salt and freshly ground black pepper, to taste

Directions:

1. Set a crockpot on High and preheat for about 25 minutes. In preheated crockpot, add all ingredients and stir to combine.

2. Set the crockpot on Low and cook, uncovered, for about 2 hours, stirring occasionally. Now, set the crockpot n High and cook, uncovered, for about 30 minutes, stirring occasionally.

3. Transfer the almonds into a bowl and set aside to cool before serving.

Nutrition:

Calories: 80

Carbohydrates: 2.9g

Protein: 2.6g

Fat: 7.1g

46.   Tastier Nuts Combo

Preparation Time: 15 minutes

Cooking Time: 2 hours

Servings: 32

Ingredients:

- 1 cup hazelnuts, toasted and skins removed

- 1 cup whole almonds, toasted

- 1 cup pecan halves, toasted

- 1 cup whole cashews

- ½ cup Erythritol

- 1/3 cup butter, melted

- ½ teaspoon ground cinnamon

- ½ teaspoon ground ginger

- ¼ teaspoon ground cloves

- ¼ teaspoon cayenne pepper

Directions:

1. In a large crockpot, add all ingredients and stir to combine. Set the crockpot on Low and cook, covered, for about 2 hours, stirring once after 1 hour.

2. Uncover the crockpot and stir nuts again. Transfer nuts onto a sheet of buttered foil to cool for at least 1 hour before serving.

Nutrition:

Calories: 101

Carbohydrates: 3.1g

Protein: 2.1g

Fat: 0.6g

CHAPTER 10:

Desserts

47.   Caramel Pear Pudding Cake

Preparation time: 15 minutes

Cooking time: 4 hours

Servings: 6

Ingredients:

- 2/3 cup all-purpose flour

- 1 teaspoon baking powder

- 1/2 cup sugar

- 1/4 teaspoon salt

- 1/2 teaspoon cinnamon powder

- 1/4 cup butter, melted

- 1/4 cup whole milk

- 4 ripe pears, cored and sliced

- 3/4 cup caramel sauce

Directions:

1. Mix the flour, baking powder, sugar, salt and cinnamon in a bowl. Add the butter and milk and give it a quick mix.

2. Place the pears in your crock pot and top with the batter. Drizzle the batter with caramel sauce and cook on low settings for 4 hours. Allow the cake to cool before serving.

Nutrition:

Calories: 210

Carbs: 25g

Fat: 11g

Protein: 4g

48.   Walnut Apple Crisp

Preparation time: 15 minutes

Cooking time: 4 hours

Servings: 6

Ingredients:

- 1 1/2 pounds Granny Smith apples, peeled, cored and sliced

- 1 teaspoon cinnamon powder

- 1 teaspoon ground ginger

- 4 tablespoons light brown sugar

- 1 tablespoon lemon juice

- 1 tablespoon cornstarch

- 1/2 cup all-purpose flour

- 1 cup ground walnuts

- 2 tablespoons white sugar

- 1 pinch salt

- 1/4 cup butter, melted

- Caramel sauce for serving

Directions:

1. Mix the apples, cinnamon, ginger, light brown sugar, lemon juice and cornstarch in your crock pot. For the topping, mix the flour, walnuts, white sugar, salt and butter in a bowl.

2. Spread this mixture over the apples and cover the pot. Cook on low settings for 4 hours. Serve the crisp chilled.

Nutrition:

Calories: 282

Carbs: 50g

Fat: 9g

Protein: 5g

49. **Crock Pot Quick Cake**

Preparation time: 15 minutes

Cooking time: 1 hour

Servings: 8

Ingredients:

- 1 tbsp Butter

- 3 tbsp almond flour

- 1 tbsp sweetener

- 1 pinch cinnamon

- 1 egg yolk

- 1/8 tsp vanilla extract

- 1 pinch salt 2 tbsp sugar-free chocolate chips

Directions:

1. Melt butter in a medium-sized pan, let it brown a little. Mix the browned butter with the mentioned amount of almond flour in a bowl.

2. Add sweetener and cinnamon. Mix everything well. Add the egg yolk, after this add vanilla extract, a pinch of salt. Add the sugar-free chocolate chips. Stir to combine.

3. Open the Crock Pot and spray a surface and sides with cooking spray or oil and place your mixture. Close the Crock Pot and put on high for an hour.

4. Once the time is over, let it cool some minutes and then dig in! Enjoy with ice cream. Bon Appetite!

Nutrition:

Calories: 275

Carbs: 12g

Fat: 10g

Protein: 10g

50. Almond Butter Fudge Bars

Preparation time: 15 minutes

Cooking time: 1 hour

Servings: 9

Ingredients:

- 1 cup almond flour

- ½ cup unsalted butter

- 6 tbsp powdered erythritol (sweetener)

- ½ tsp ground cinnamon

- ¼ cup heavy cream

- ½ cup almond butter

- ½ tsp vanilla extract

- 1/8 tsp xanthan gum

- 1 oz 80% dark chocolate or sugar-free chocolate chips

Directions:

1. Open the Crock Pot and spread the cooking spray over the sides and the bottom. Melt the butter and divide into portions.

2. In a medium-sized bowl whisk together almond flour, melted butter, powdered erythritol, cinnamon. Combine everything well.

3. Spread the mixture on the bottom of the Crock-Pot, cover and set on high for 1 hour. The mixture must get golden brown.

4. Take off the almond base and let it cool. Chop the dark chocolate finely. Whisk together in a large bowl heavy cream with almond butter, remained butter and powdered erythritol.

5. Add the vanilla and xanthan gum and blend everything well. Spread the mixture over the cooled almond base and sprinkle with chopped dark chocolate or if desired with chocolate chips.

6. Freeze overnight, slice the base into bars and serve. Enjoy!

Nutrition:

Calories: 240

Carbs: 12g Fat: 15g

Conclusion

You have to the end of this amazing cookbook, but always remember that this is not the end of your cooking journey with the crockpot; but instead, this is your stepping stone towards more cooking glory. We hope you have found your favorite recipes that are time-saving and money-saving.

Now that you know how Crockpot works and the many benefits of using it, maybe it is time for you to buy one for your family, in case you haven't owned one. When it comes to time spent preparing meals for your family, Crock-Pot is a lifesaver. If you are a busy person, a powerful solution is to use the crockpot.

You will also love to own one if you want to make your life simpler at work if you want to make your life simpler at home, and if you want to preserve some of the natural resources. You could also use one if you want to lean towards a healthier lifestyle as cooking in the crockpot is conducive to health than in the oven.

The crockpot can be used in making homemade and custom-made buffets, even in catering services. You can use it for cooking for your staff for special occasions and for showing them how to cook a tasty and healthier dish for your guests well within their own crockpot.

After choosing the best one for you, maybe it is time for you to know more about the recipes you should use. There are various recipes in this cookbook that are perfect for crockpot cooking, and they will definitely be useful and beneficial for you.

Moreover, whether you are a newbie or an experienced cook, you are going to love this cookbook as it is packed with every conceivable taste. You have discovered more than 1000 recipes in this cookbook that you can put into practice using your crockpot. You can always customize the recipes to suit your taste buds, as you can make any recipe mild or hot, sweet or sour; you have all the freedom to make the recipes your own. The best thing about cooking using a crockpot is that you just need to add the main ingredients, and no other complicated cooking preparation is needed; the crockpot will add most of the other ingredients for you.

This crockpot cookbook covered all the recipes that are sure to make your heart happy and your taste buds happy as well. These meals are not just easy to make, but they will also save you hours of preparation and cleanup. The crockpot is also famous for its great nutritional value. It is the best nutritional value you will ever get. The high levels of healthy fats, proteins, and fiber you get when you cook using the crockpot are entirely natural, which everybody needs. Some of the ingredients are healthy enough to be consumed on their own.

When you are done with the crockpot recipes, just store them and access them whenever you need to. You could use them for a party, and your guests will love the recipes. They will love your attention to detail and your hospitality. You can invite them over, and when they are all set to leave, you will say that you must give them something of yours that you hope they will like, and now you know what recipes to include in such a thought that they will love and appreciate.

The only limit of the crockpot is your imagination and creativity. That is definitely why you fell in love with the crockpot. That is why you are going to expand your love for the crockpot through all these recipes.

After cooking with these recipes, you are sure that there are so many advantages of cooking with the crockpot. With all that said, use these recipes, and you will see that cooking is much easier than you have ever imagined it and that cooking can be fun as well. Go ahead and put your own signature twist on these recipes and let these recipes add magic to your life.

CPSIA information can be obtained
at www.ICGtesting.com
Printed in the USA
BVHW041733220421
605649BV00010B/260